A pad and a pen

Nat gets a pen.

4

Nat gets a pad.

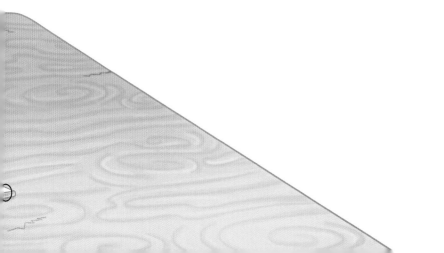

A red hen is
on the pad.

A fat rat is
on the pad.

A big bus is
on the pad.

Sid taps the pen.

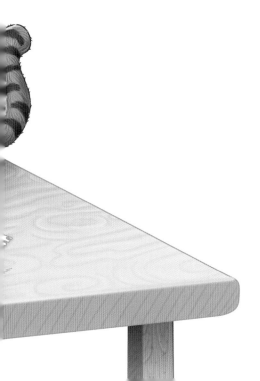

Sid is on the pad.

A pad and a pen

Before reading

Say the sounds: g o b h e r f u l

Ensure the children use the pure sounds for the consonants without the added "uh" sound, e.g. "llll" not "luh".

Practise blending the sounds: hen pad fat red bus rat pen taps gets Sid Nat

High-frequency words: and on big

Tricky words: is the no

Vocabulary check: tap – Revisit the meaning of "tap" as a noun and as a verb.

Story discussion: Look at the cover. What do you think Nat is going to do with the pad and the pen?

Teaching points: "s" is added to "get" and "tap" to make "gets" and "taps". The addition of "s" to a verb shows who is doing the action, e.g. I get, Nat gets. Review the use of speech bubbles to show what a character is saying.

After reading

Comprehension:
- What did Nat draw on the pad?
- What did Sid do to upset Nat?
- Why do you think Sid did that?

Fluency: Speed read the words again from the inside front cover.